FINCH FILES

Short Stories from a Chi-Town Englewood Blogger

ANTONIUS E. FINCH

S.H.E. PUBLISHING, LLC

FINCH FILES

Copyright © 2021 by Antonius E. Finch.

All rights reserved. Printed in the United States of America. No part of this book may be used or reproduced in any manner whatsoever without written permission except in the case of brief quotations embodied in critical articles or reviews.

For information contact:

W : www.shepublishingllc.com

E : info@shepublishingllc.com

Book and Cover design by

Michelle Phillips of CHELLD3 3D Visualization and Design

ISBN:

978-1-953163-11-0 (Paperback)

978-1-953163-12-7 (*She*Edition)

First Edition : May 2021

10 9 8 7 6 5 4 3 2 1

DEDICATION

This book is dedicated to my two sons, TJ and Anius, and my precious daughter Avery. They have been my daily inspiration and motivation. Failure is not an option because those three depend on me.

I also dedicate this book to my parents: my mom, who is a strong woman. She has overcome all of the trials and tribulations she's faced, and my dad, because he always told me he wanted to write a book about his life. Although he is not with us today and never fulfilled that wish, consider me checking this goal off on both of our bucket lists.

CONTENTS

- MEN IN **RELATIONSHIPS** 1
- BLACK **LOVE** IS AN ENDANGERED SPECIES 7
- WEIRD **FEELINGS** 11
- FOREVER **BREEZY** 15
- JUNKIE 4 **SUCCESS** 19
- **CHRISTINA** PT. 1 23
- **NFL** 27
- DATE **NIGHT** WITH MY CRUSH 31
- THE **PURSUIT** OF HAPPINESS 35
- RELATED NOT **FAMILY** 41
- **JEALOUSY** 45
- LOVE **EXPERIENCE** 51
- DIFFERENCE IN **DEATH** 55
- DOMESTIC **VIOLENCE** 61
- **SNITCHING** 67
- ADVICE FOR **WOMEN** 71
- 2014 A YEAR TO **FORGET** 77
- ROAD TO **RICHES** 83
- DEADLIEST DAY IN **CHICAGO** IN OVER A DECADE 89
- **ACKNOWLEDGMENTS** 93

FINCH FILES

Short Stories from a Chi-Town Englewood Blogger

ANTONIUS E. FINCH

MEN IN RELATIONSHIPS

Antonius Finch

MEN IN RELATION SHIPS

LET ME BEGIN BY SAYING THAT THIS IS A CONTROVERSIAL topic, one that will spark different reactions and emotions from the public. I'm writing this using my experience (The Good, The Bad, The Truth)!

What is the role of a man in a relationship? What level of respect should the man have for his mate? How do you determine when to walk away or when to stay and fight?

I was taught that a man is to provide and always be the source of strength for his family. There is a term that is used loosely, "what's understood don't have to be explained." That phrase needs to be eliminated from our vocabulary. That phrase is the precise reason that there are so many dysfunctional relationships.

Communication is key. I don't see an issue with discussing roles, expectations and responsibilities in relationships. Musiq Soulchild's first verse in "Teach Me" is powerful. It is as quoted below:

I was told the true definition of a man was never to cry
Work tilou tired (yeah), got to provide (yeah)
Always be the rock for my fam', protect them by all means
   (and give you the things that you need, baby)

What happens when a man is doing that, and it is still not enough to satisfy his mate? What happens when everything is going great, and the mate commits infidelity? Some people cheat for no reason.

What happens when a woman is not submissive or supportive and is constantly challenging his leadership qualities? At some point, that man has seen his efforts go unappreciated, and now that woman has made it difficult for the man to lead.

Men don't fall in love often, but when they do, and it's not reciprocated, a beast can be unleashed. If he pays the bill, does he have to compromise? If he catches her cheating and takes her back, is it his turn? If she brings kids into the relationship and the father is a deadbeat, does he have the right to force her to put him on child support?

First off, there is a shortage of men for women to select from. This has given men an advantage in the dating realm. There are plenty of women that don't mind being #2. If you are an independent man and can hold a conversation, meeting a woman is no problem.

Jay Z and R Kelly released one of the best albums of all time. On that album is a song called "The Power of the P-U-$-$-Y." "The chorus of that song is true!"

> The power of the P-U-$-$-Y,
> Thatz why every mutherfucka in the world dress fly.
> Every baller that can afford it they cop the best ride, for the power of the P-U-$-$-Y.
> (Let's have some fun)
> The power of the P-U-$-$-Y, thatz why niggaz get they hair cut, try to dress fly.
> Every baller that can afford it he cop the best ride.
> For the Power of the P-U-$-$-Y.

Some women have the same mentality as men. They enjoy casual sex with multiple partners. Unfortunately, the world that we live in has double standards. In my opinion, a woman is supposed to hold value to her body. Her body is not to be explored by nearly every male that she dates. If a woman doesn't value herself, why should a man?

I have been in situations with women involved in relationships that were attracted to me or to what they perceived to be my lifestyle, and they gave their body to me. After we would spend 2-3 hours together, they would go back home to their mate. After experiencing this with multiple women, I realized some people are heartless. I had to take a look at myself and realize I was wrong. I held myself to a higher standard, but I wanted to be on the other end of the totem pole after experiencing my own heartache.

What are your opinions? Please define the role of a man! Women, remember that if every man has had you, you go from being a prize to a thing to do!

    Respectfully,
    Antonius Finch

Antonius Finch

BLACK LOVE IS AN ENDANGERED SPECIES

Antonius Finch

BLACK **LOVE** is an ENDANGERED SPECIES

BLACK LOVE IS AN ENDANGERED SPECIES! BLACK LOVE IS an *Endangered Species!* Black Love Is an Endangered Species!

Gone, will be the backbone of families (grandparents)! Our culture will be lost, and our history will be told by people that have no genetic connection with our journey. You may ask, what has caused the breakage in the African American community? It is the lack of fathers. This problem has caused an epidemic that has spiraled out of control.

This is not a book about saving our youth. I believe that topic has generated plenty of discussions, articles, town halls and debates on how to do that. This is about the vulnerable African American woman. This is about how the Black male has failed her. This is about how we force stress upon them because of their loyalty to us. This is about how we forget that they need compassion and love as well.

I want to state that I believe in love. I believe that each person should have the right to marry or date anyone regardless of race or religion. However, I believe that African American men will continue being murdered and incarcerated at the current pace that black women may have to seek alternative dating options. Suppose our women are breeding an interracial baby, that is diminishing the African American population. It is staggering when you look at the statistics. African Americans make up 15% of the state's population, but makeup 60% of the prison population. In total, 873,686 African American men reside in Illinois, while 992,728 African American women reside in Illinois. More women graduate college and climb the Corporate America ladder than men. They have fewer options to select from the further they travel up the success ladder.

When we say 'Black Lives Matter', there should be a subtitle that says, 'Black Families Matter'. Once we strengthen the Black families, we will continue to raise productive children. We will secure our futures and become positive role models for our children, family and peers. Any suggestions on how we can do this? We have to protect our women.

Respectfully,
Antonius E. Finch

Antonius Finch

WEIRD FEELINGS

WEIRD **FEELINGS**

WHEN POP DIED, DIDN'T CRY/DIDN'T KNOW HIM THAT WELL.

Between him doing heroin and me doing crack sells......
Quote from Jay Z!

Pop, I forgive you for all the shit I lived through. It wasn't all your fault you got caught to the same game I fought, that Uncle Black originally lost. I'm just glad we got to see each other/talk and re-meet each other. Save a place in Heaven until we meet again forever!

The call came at 4:20 p.m. I was nearing the end of my workday. Damn, I just lost a parent. I was confused because I wasn't sure how I felt. I was sad that he was gone. I was angry because he left two adolescent daughters behind. I was pissed because his love for his children wasn't strong enough to combat his habit; however, I was glad that he wasn't in any more pain!

I remember the ride to Fort Wayne. Thank God for the passenger. That trip brought me closer to reality. My grandfather is deceased, and my dad is dead. I'm on the clock. Life has a peculiar way of making you face reality and do an account overview of your entire life.

I thought about all of the trips we made together, hitting the highway running the sack up. If it goes bad, Pops said, he was standing tall. Wow, he showed his love the only way he knew how. Sometimes I look to the sky, trying to make eye contact with a star. Every star reminds me of a memory that we have. Good and bad. I wish we had more time to build memories.

    Respectfully,
    Antonius E. Finch

Antonius Finch

FF
FOREVER BREEZY

Antonius Finch

FOREVER **BREEZY**

WAKE UP EVERYBODY, THE SHIFT IN THE WIND IS STRONG.
The chill is so intense that you feel it in your bones!

If you think I'm talking about the weather, you are dead wrong. I'm referring to January 13, 2017, when Bang Bang was summoned home!

The spirit of the youth has the city nervous.
This structural breakdown was designed on purpose!
Of course, I'm supporting the stop of the violence movement.

The L's I throw up represent Long Live Lewis!
An innocent kid killed by demonic people.
Just trying to spread love in a world so filled with evil.
Some are walking with their eyes open, but no vision.
As they accepted, their final destination is a graveyard or prison.

We need Jesus now; please believe me!

"Church off in these streets"; sleep well, #ForeverBreezy!

    P.S.
    We Love You Kierra
    Antonius E. Finch

Antonius Finch

JUNKIE 4 SUCCESS

JUNKIE 4 **SUCCESS**

When did I become a 'Junkie 4 Success'???
It was May 3rd, 2003, to be exact;
Let me explain...

SINCE BIRTH, I HAVE ALWAYS WANTED TO WIN. ALTHOUGH I was born into a bad situation (16-year-old mother and a dad in the streets), I was showered with lots of love. My grandfather instilled being a winner in me at an early age. Success is measured by your personal thought of victories. Early in life, it was winning a race, playing basketball, earning excellent grades, out thinking my guys, winning a fight, etc. However, the day I became a 'Junkie 4 Success' changed my life FOREVER!

I walked in the door, and my mom gave me a message; I was shocked. So many thoughts rushed through my mind. I recognized the name on the message. I knew who this person was connected to. I contemplated for all of 10 seconds before picking up the phone. I was already addicted before the first conversation. I knew if I picked up the phone, there was no turning back.

We started with humble beginnings. A bus ride to the Orange Line. A kiss on the Kedzie train platform. Every second, every interaction, every memory, I inhaled Success more. The road to ultimate Success comes with a lot of lessons. I would never call them losses.

Our motto was:
We gon' take it to the Moon, take it to the stars
How many people you know can take it this far?
I'm supercharged
I'm bout to take this whole thing to Mars
Now we gon' take it to the Moon, take it to the stars
You don't know what we been through, to make it this far
So many scars
'Bout to take this whole thing to Mars

Life is funny. I have always been a 'Junkie 4 Success'!

    Respectfully,
    Antonius E. Finch

Antonius Finch

CHRISTINA PT. 1

CHRISTINA Pt. 1

I HAVE SEEN CHRISTINA IN CLOTHES. THE GRAY TAPE WITH the X in the middle. I took my time undressing her. Every ounce is precious, and I want it all. I dreamed about caressing her all over, using my hands to make sure she is authentic. I have placed her love in my mouth until she released her scent. I put my finger in her center and run it around my gums until I'm satisfied with this potent product. I had to bag her. I had to strengthen the fabulous 4 (mentally, spiritually, sexually and submissiveness). Break her down to a nine-piece in order to make her stronger and more complete, 4 of them to be exact. I had to make her cold to the past, so she had to spend some time in the freezer.

All she needed was love and affection. This is what hustlers call Superior B. I had to flatten her out; squeeze all of the impurities out. When people see her, they see me and I'm accustomed to the finer things. Break her down to remove the scent of her past. Pick up a piece, and I can look and see this is my diamond. I got nothing but glass. At the end of the day, the return on my investment has made me a richer man. Richer, in the same ways, I improved her. Mentally, Spiritually, Sexually and Submissively.

P.S. A man's success has a lot to do with the woman he chooses to build a castle with.

P.S. If you can't get it 100% potent, keep that $36,000 in the safe……….

>Respectfully,
>Antonius E. Finch

Antonius Finch

NFL

OVER THE PAST TWO WEEKS, WE HAVE WITNESSED NFL player, coaches and owners take a knee to protest. Some people believe that is a sign of solidarity and unity. I agree that it is a sign of solidarity and unity. My only questions are, 'What protest is kneeling for?' 'What was the urgent matter that the **NFL** had to show solidarity and unity for?'

We all know that it wasn't to protest the police shootings of unarmed African American men. We all know that it wasn't to protest the inequality in prison sentences between African American men and Caucasian men. We all know that it wasn't for the right to exercise our rights under the Constitution of the United States of America. Last but not least, we all know that it wasn't in support of their colleague, **Colin Kaepernick**.

Everything that the **NFL's** show of strength didn't represent, **Kaepernick** took a kneel for. The only way to orchestrate change is to create uncomfortable situations. **Kaepernick's** actions will always be one of the most prominent demonstrations against the oppressor. Do you understand what this means he sacrificed? He gambled with his career. He has been "blackballed" (I hate that term) from the **NFL**.

The **NFL's** show of unity and solidarity was against **Donald Trump**. They were upset that he tried to tell them how to run their business. After some players saw how **Colin Kaepernick** was being shunned **by the NFL**, they took the cautious route and protested in their minds. They didn't protest with their actions. They shouldn't have protested at all. I always thought the **NFL** stood for **National Football League**, but I truly understand that it stands for **Niggas for Life**.

    Respectfully,
    Antonius E. Finch

Antonius Finch

DATE NIGHT WITH MY CRUSH

DATE **NIGHT** with MY CRUSH

SO MUCH ANTICIPATION. SO MUCH MENTAL AND physical preparation. I had the date planned out from start to finish. There was just one problem. She didn't know she was going yet. I thought of so many different ways to ask her out. I tried to prepare myself for whatever her response would be. This took a lot of thought; this took a lot of courage. After all, this had been my crush since the late '90s.

The concert was approaching. Time was against me. I remember the phone call; heart beating fast. Wait, I'm Smooth; this should come naturally. However, this is not an ordinary lady. This is a one-off. This is a rarity. There is no one else like her. When I asked her, she seemed shocked, but it was in the atmosphere. Shockingly, she accepted.

I called my grandmother and talked to her. She advised me to keep it simple. The day of the concert was an adventure. She had a few twists and turns, but she put forth the effort and came. When she got out of her car and started walking in my direction, I was stunned. A natural beauty. No fake hair, no fake body parts, no fake nails. She is all authentic, and I love it.

When I gave her flowers, she was shocked. She couldn't wait to take a picture of it; we were trying to feel each other out. While driving, I inhaled and realized I was living in the midst of my fantasy. I decided to take it all in. In her words, "Good times with Good People" was the motto for the night. I loved being her personal photographer for the evening. My crush is the bomb, and our first date was everything. Lady L. we must do this again, real soon!

Respectfully,
Antonius E. Finch

Antonius Finch

THE PURSUIT OF HAPPINESS

Antonius Finch

THE PURSUIT
of HAPPINESS

IS THIS SOMETHING THAT YOU ARE DOING? HOW WOULD you describe happiness? As we evolve, our concept of happiness evolves also. I asked myself, what is happiness?

Happiness used to be crossing a defender over on the basketball court at Murray Park, playing Double Dribble on Nintendo, eating McDonald's, winning a race, getting good grades and seeing my mom and grandparents' smile. That is what happiness was to me as a child.

As a high school teenager, happiness was playing basketball all day during summer break, going school clothes shopping with my mom, walking and talking with a girl, going to the movies and homecoming, getting butterflies before running on the court for high school basketball, getting good grades and seeing my mom and granny smile.

As a college student, happiness was starting at the point

guard position on a college basketball team. The joy was traveling state to state and being adored by college basketball fanatics. The pleasure was hearing my family brag about me being in college and paving a bright path for my future. However, during my college years, my happiness changed for the worse.

After my brother, Shawn Esco, was murdered, my **Pursuit of Happiness** was revenge. My happiness centered on evening the score. A demonic force now overtook my happiness. I reminisce on that era in my life, and I realize how blessed I am. At the exact moment I was prepared to throw my life away, my first son was born. This wasn't an ordinary birth; it was an extraordinary birth. He was born on my birthday. That shifted my **Pursuit of Happiness**.

As a young adult, my happiness centered around a four-letter word: L-O-V-E. The love a father shares for his first child and the love a man shares for a woman; the love I have for my younger brother as he was beginning to blossom into a young man. I'm 15 years his senior. I experienced happiness a second time when my youngest son was born.

As I look back on my life as a young adult, I realize that I was stuck in an identity crisis. I was heartbroken due to the death of my brother; I was heartbroken because I didn't achieve my dream of playing in the NBA. I wanted to live that lifestyle while not having that career. I had a beautiful woman who had never understood the meaning of loyalty as far as I'm concerned. So, my **Pursuit of Happiness** ended.

Fortunately, I was able to identify with myself, and that is when I realized I never had to pursue happiness because happiness is whatever I make it. Once we realize that happiness doesn't have a destination or a specific income, once we understand that satisfaction doesn't drive a specific vehicle or reside in a certain neighborhood, we will realize that we are happy. Are you in **The Pursuit of Happiness**?

    Prayers for Lamar Odom
    Antonius E. Finch

Antonius Finch

RELATED NOT FAMILY

Antonius Finch

RELATED NOT FAMILY

RELATED NOT FAMILY! WHAT IS THE FIRST THING THAT comes to mind? It may be positive; it may be negative, or you simply may be confused. Personally, this **statement is powerful**. Truth is more potent than any drug. As I write this, I can't help but think about everyone that I'm related to. I suddenly realized we are related, but we are not family.

Related is an adjective that means, "*belonging to the same family, group or type; connected.*"

Family is a noun that means "*a basic social unit consisting of parents and their children, considered as a group, rather dwelling or not.*"

Family: Any group of people closely related by blood, as parents, children, uncles, aunts and cousins.

Family: All people considered as descendants of a common progenitor or members of the same community.

After I read the definitions, I understood that "**BLOOD**"

makes us RELATED, but it does not make us FAMILY. Hate, jealousy, evil thoughts, demonic spirits are things that *FAMILY does not harbor and procreate for future generations.* I have *"BLOOD"* relatives that I no longer consider *FAMILY* and *some that I have never considered FAMILY.*

I have *"BLOOD"* connections on both of my parents' sides that I don't consider family. After *many incidents* and *over time*, I have decided that *RELATED AND FAMILY have two different meanings.* If we are trying to *enhance one another, can celebrate one another's accomplishments and can show each other unconditional love*, that is what I deem meaningful. *I don't want to interact or engage with anyone that is not pure in my heart toward me*. I don't feel comfortable associating with them, and *I make all attempts to limit interaction.* In most cases, eliminating contact will reduce any physical altercations and provide distance and space for the Lord to intervene. *Hopefully, this will make us a family again.*

Controversial topics tend to have powerful discussions....

Respectively,
Antonius E. Finch

Antonius Finch

JEALOUSY

JEALOUSY

JEALOUSY IS A SEED THAT IS PLANTED AND ROOTED IN those with low self-esteem, hatred, ignorance, selfishness and envy. When you are JEALOUS of a person, it simply means that you wish you were that person. You wish that your children grow up and have more traits similar to that person than you. JEALOUSY is the personal feeling that your star is completely overshadowed by the mere thought or presence of a specific individual.

I can honestly say that I have never been JEALOUS of anyone. There are people that I think are awesome. I look at their success, and I think of how their success can influence me. I don't feel emptiness; I feel motivated. I'm humble enough to give acclamation to them and ask for any tips that can lead me to greener pastures while remaining morally ethical.

There are two types of JEALOUSY. One type is from afar. That type of JEALOUSY has no solid basis. This is what you call "on the outside looking in". This is JEALOUSY through assumptions. This is what you expect from people who don't know you.

The worse form of JEALOUSY is from FAMILY/FRIENDS. This is detrimental because it hurts you to your core, especially when you have encouraged them and, in some cases, nurtured them. It is extremely painful when it is someone that you looked up to. These are the most dangerous people in your life. You may detect the JEALOUSY, but you turn a blind eye out of disbelief and love. Sometimes, people are forced to deal with reality. The reality of the situation is simply: We all make decisions, and we all have to live and die by our decisions.

Below are some quotes from Jay Z, concerning JEALOUSY:

People see you at events and pretend to be friendly, but I know that any success breeds envy!

Trapped, everyone is against me, in fact, but ain't no turning back; bring it on.

Hate the price of success because it cost too much; can I live without saying I floss too much?

Hate the way you make this hate flow all through us; steady looking for flaws through us. Lucky Me!

I wish success to everyone. I want to see everyone prosper. So I will leave on this note:

JEALOUSY is a weak emotion.

If you are JEALOUS person, you are just a weak mother….. The Mad Rapper!

    Respectfully,
    Antonius E. Finch

Antonius Finch

LOVE EXPERIENCE

Antonius Finch

LOVE EXPERIENCE

IF I COULD, I WOULD TAKE BACK EVERY LIE I TOLD. I WOULD have wiped her tears when she cried. I wouldn't have embarrassed her on New Years by not answering her call at Midnight! I would have been by her side. I would have cut ties with a dead relationship. I would make love to her with intensity and passion. I would kiss her deeply, look in her eyes and tell her how much I'm in love with her. My messenger would have been a virgin. Instead, I did none of this, and now I'm faced with a reality that I don't want, but I'm forced to accept.

I knew how much she cared, and I know how reckless it was to pray for something and not realize when you have your blessing. I wasn't in control of my flesh, but she owned my heart and mind. If I had another week, one more day, just an hour or another second, the story would be totally different. Hopefully, the final chapter isn't complete. From matching shirts to matching shoes, it was always meant to be her and Smooth. One more Divvy Bike Ride. Eddie Vs, and London House, Sweetest Day; girl, you are all I need!

A dramatic life event made me take a deep look in the mirror. I became a mature man overnight. I always knew what was right. I realized how selfish I was. I realized how much this woman meant to me. I realized how hurt I would be if she ever left. I called her phone, and it wasn't blocked, but my calls went unanswered. Suddenly, I thought of every lie, every disappointment and every tear. I started calling her family and friends, begging for them to tell her to give me another chance. I was ready to be the man that she deserved and the man she knew I could be. That opportunity never came!

This is a message to the men: Don't make this mistake. In a world filled with materialistic and superficial women, please have the vision and wisdom to recognize when you have a real woman on your team. Fellas: understand that her heart is delicate, but her loyalty is deep. Please know that you are not the only man who wants her. Don't be left on the outside looking in.

Love is a powerful addiction. Embrace the moment and create dope memories.

    Respectfully,
    Antonius Finch

Antonius Finch

DIFFERENCE IN DEATH

DIFFERENCE IN DEATH

What is death? Is there a difference in death?

Death is when someone's *earthly life* has ended. Yes, in my opinion, *there is a difference in death*!

I'M USING ALL FACTS TO SUPPORT MY THEORY. MY *grandfather **died on January 22, 1994***. His death literally destroyed my family. Although my **grandmother is a great person**, it was my grandfather that **set the rules, protected and enforced them without prejudice.** Unfortunately, there wasn't a lot of advancement in cancer research, and doctors were inexperienced. I believe this was when the medical field was **using senior citizens as guinea pigs** for the advancement of medicine.

My grandfather was ***diagnosed with cancer in June 1993, and he died in January 1994.*** It gave us ***time to prepare*** for his transition to Grace. We went to the hospital appointments and took turns staying at the hospital. He was never alone. It established bonds and, for a moment, brought the family together.

Contrary to this form of death, is ***sudden death***. This type ***surprises you.*** I will ***never forget that Thursday night*** when I received the news ***about my brother, Shawn***. I will ***never forget that midday call on Tuesday about Kashif***. I will ***never forget the early morning text I received about Prime being shot and the phone call a few hours later that he passed***. I will ***never forget my dad. I was driving down Damen Street and I blew my car horn at S. Dot as a greeting. By the time we made it to 73rd & Paulina, we had heard the shots.*** Those were sudden. ***I didn't have a chance to say goodbye***.

Shawn was scheduled to ***visit that week and stay with me in my apartment on my college campus. I*** was supposed to see ***Young Jeezy perform that night at Hearts with Kashif***. I just ***walked with Prime two days earlier at the same time to the place where he died (Johns). His death haunts me*** because he walked to Johns two days later with my dad and ***never made it back*** to the block. What if ***evil was lurking*** that fateful ***Halloween night in 1999*** when I walked to the ***New Attitude*** and ***couldn't get in because I didn't have my ID?*** What if **evil was lurking when Kashif and I were riding in the VW sipping Ro'se talking about kids, cars, women and money a week earlier?** What if ***evil was lurking when Prime and I walked to Johns 2 days earlier at the same time? What if evil was lurking when I turned the corner and blew the horn at S Dot?***

Death hurts no matter how it occurs, but sudden death has a way of being more ***demoralizing and more demonic. I pray that we don't experience any sudden death this year as a family, a community, a city, a state, a nation, a world and a universe.***

Respectfully,
Antonius Finch

Antonius Finch

DOMESTIC VIOLENCE

DOMESTIC VIOLENCE

WHAT ARE YOUR INITIAL THOUGHTS WHEN YOU ARE informed of a **Domestic Violence** issue? I have the image of a man being physically abusive with a woman. That is simply one method. Below is a list of categories that all **Domestic Violence** altercations can be categorized in.

The different types of **Domestic Violence** are:

> Physical

Inflicting or attempting to inflict physical injury.
Example: grabbing, pinching, shoving, slapping, hitting, biting, arm-twisting, kicking, punching, hitting with blunt objects, stabbing, shooting.
Withholding access to resources necessary to maintain health. Example: medication, medical care, wheelchair, food or fluids, sleep, hygienic assistance forcing alcohol or another drug use.

Psychological

Instilling or attempting to instill fear. Example: intimidation, threatening physical harm to the self, victim or others, threatening to harm or kidnap children, menacing, blackmail, harassment, destructtion of pets and property, mind games, stalking.

Isolating or attempting to isolate the victim from friends, family, school or work. Example: withholding access to phone or transportation, undermining victim's personal relationships, harassing others, constant "checking up," constant accompaniment, use of unfounded accusations, forced imprisonment.

Sexual

Coercing or attempting to coerce any sexual contact without consent. Example: marital rape, acquaintance rape, forced sex after the physical beating, attacks on the sexual parts of the body, forced prostitution, fondling, sodomy, sex with others.

Attempting to undermine the victim' sexuality. Example: treating him/her in a sexually derogatory manner, criticizing sexual performance and desirability, accusations of infidelity, withholding sex.

Emotional

Undermining or attempting to undermine the victim's sense of worth. Example: constant criticism, belittling the victim's abilities and competency, name-calling, insults, put-downs, silent treatment, manipulating the victim's feelings and emotions to induce guilt, subverting a partner's relationship with the children, repeatedly making and breaking promises.

Economic

Making or attempting to make the victim financially dependent. Example: maintaining total control over financial resources including the victim's earned income or resources received through public assistance or social security, withholding money or access to money, forbidding attendance at school, forbidding employment, on-the-job harassment, requiring accountability and justification for all money spent, forced welfare fraud, withholding information about a family running up bills for which the victim is responsible for payment.

What are your thoughts?

Respectfully,
Antonius E. Finch

Antonius Finch

FT SNITCHING

SNITCHING

SNITICHING............ IS A CONTROVERSIAL TOPIC. SOME people are against it, while some people are advocates. Some people say they are against it, but will use it as a bargaining tool when they find themselves in violation of the law. Some people are successful in their criminal endeavors because they are confidential informants (snitches). The first thing we have to do is define snitching.

> Snitch: Inform on someone

Is snitching ever ok? Is snitching wrong? As children in urban communities, we are taught not to be a 'tattletale'. As a child, we all snitched on our siblings, cousins and friends. We understood early in our adolescent years that no one likes to get in trouble. However, people have to take accountability for their actions. In everything we do, we have to understand the consequences of our actions.

Example 1: If we agree to commit a crime together and during or after the crime is committed, I get caught. Should I tell on my partner? My personal opinion on this situation is NO. I will not speak on my partner because I understood before the crime was committed that a possibility existed that I may be caught and would have to face whatever reprimands followed.

Example 2: If we agree to play basketball at a local gym and during our travel, the passenger sees a person that he doesn't like, exits my vehicle and murders someone, and I'm arrested. Do you tell on the shooter? My personal opinion on this situation is YES. It is an unwritten rule that if we see a common, known neighborhood threat (opp) and a crime is committed that I automatically support it (if that is the life I chose), but if I didn't choose that life, I refuse to take the blame for another man's actions.

What is your opinion? What are your thoughts? Feel free to comment!

Respectfully,
Antonius E. Finch

Antonius Finch

ADVICE FOR WOMEN

ADVICE FOR **WOMEN**

WHAT DOES EVERY MAN WANT IN A RELATIONSHIP? I CAN'T speak for every man, but I will tell you the basics. A man wants a God-fearing, loyal, honest, supportive, understanding, ambitious, confident and sexually experimental woman. I understand that you have to be what you are looking for.

Some women have had three boyfriends in 6 months. They post pictures with all three on social media and proclaim their love for them. They shower them with praise because that is the image they want to portray— not realizing that they are marketing themselves as an easy score for anyone with a conversation and who can put forward a decent presentation.

Some women don't understand that in order to be successful in this world, you have to think like a man, but act like a woman. There is a double standard in the world, which I have to disagree with. I believe a woman should be paid just as much as a man, if not more, based on education, experience and job performance. I'm not a sexist.

It's a preconceived notion that boys are taught to "turn nothing down but their collar." That is the status quo among heterosexual males. As an adult, I realize that thinking in that barbaric manner is wrong. I believe sex should be shared among consenting adults. However, it is my opinion that a woman should be more selective with whom she gives her body.

Some women would rather deal with a man who is more likely to deal with multiple women than a man who will give her the world or work mercilessly to try. If a man is attractive, fun, exciting, handsome, God-fearing, educated and in love with you, what more could you want? No one is perfect, but what do you think? Do some women have a hard time understanding when she is winning because "SHE IS USED TO LOSING."

I have had encounters with beautiful women with all of the extras. However, I tell them all what good is the bonus without the basics. Seriously, imagine fixing a sandwich. You have the Italian bread and all of the condiments that will make this sandwich tasty. That is the extra. Suddenly, you realize you don't have the basics. That is the lunch meat. How can a man appreciate the perks when the basics are not there?

You have a relationship with every person that is in your life. The extent of the relationship depends on the people involved. With that in mind, women: forget this new age madness and choose a mate that you believe in, a mate that inspires you, a mate that makes you feel sexy, a mate that you know loves you and a mate you know wants and doesn't need you. Remember being God-fearing, loyal, honest, supportive, understanding, ambitious, confident and sexually experimental is the key. A man does not want a woman who knows all the men. A man wants a woman that he can grow with! Ladies/gentlemen, do you agree? Please feel free to comment.

Respectfully,
Antonius E. Finch

Antonius Finch

FF
2014
A YEAR TO FORGET

2014 – A YEAR TO FORGET

JANUARY 1, 2014, THE YEAR STARTED AS A BLANK SHEET OF paper. It was up to us to write the story. Unfortunately, the book that was written was not one that needed an encore. 2014 was highlighted by violence. This time, violence came knocking at my front door.

First, let me begin by listing the **top 10 communities** in Illinois with the most homicides:

Englewood (49), Austin (36), Garfield Park (33), Humboldt Park (25), Chicago Lawn (20), Chatham (18), Auburn Gresham (18), South Shore (16), South Chicago (15), New City (15).

Needless to say, I'm extremely frustrated that my community leads the pack. It is frustrating because the city frowns upon everyone from these communities. This is when the cliche "One bad apple can ruin a bunch" becomes precedent.

I have to honor the memories of those that we lost to gun violence that I knew personally. I knew some better than others, but **these nine homicide victims have touched my life, as well as the lives of those I care for.** So let me say, **"Father forgive them because they all have sinned, but they are all good men, so please let them in."** I have to honor them by giving them a special mention:

1. Kashif Tillis
2. Michael Clark Sr.
3. Shaquille "S Dot" Holmes
4. Ryan Pargo
5. Deandre Baber
6. Jerel Goodman
7. Tony McIntosh
8. Demarcus Boswell
9. Kevin Roberson

These statistics are alarming: 78.1% of all homicide victims were African American, 14.8% Hispanic and 7.1%

white/other. That is an alarming rate for minorities. *A person was shot in Chicago every 3 hours 19 minutes, and a person was killed in Chicago every 19 hours and 12 minutes on average in 2014. Are these odds in our favor?*

The deadliest age range is **18-24**, followed by **25-34** and **0-17**. The **deadliest days in 2014 were the weekend**. Fridays experienced 78 homicides, while Saturdays had 82 and Sundays had 83. The Police wounded 28 people, and shot and killed 17 people. We had a **total of 456 murder victims**, and 411 of them were male, and 45 were female. Below is a list of all of the different types of murder in 2014: *How many of us fit this criterion? How many of us have loved ones that fit this criterion as well*?

Gunshot (388) 85%, Stabbing (33) 7.2%, Assault (16) 3.5%, Auto (8) 1.8%, Child Abuse (5) 1.1%, Strangulation (3) 0.7% Arson (2) 0.4% and Neglect (1) 0.2%.

How can we raise a positive society in these conditions? How can we improve? HELP!

Respectfully,
Antonius Finch

Antonius Finch

ROAD TO RICHES

ROAD TO
RICHES

THERE IS NO BLUEPRINT FOR SUCCESS. HOWEVER, THERE are **specific characteristics** that are needed. This book depicts but also support my personal opinion. **As parents, it is our job to provide opportunities for our children to be successful. Our job is to ensure a safe and stable atmosphere for our children to blossom and maximize their life advantages.**

Case Study #1: A child that grows up in a two-parent household in an upper-middle-class neighborhood. Both of his or her parents are successful members of society. He or she never had to work for anything. He or she never had to suffer or go without. He or she never understood what the bottom feels like. Is that good, or is that bad? Is he or she supposed to experience that? He or she is destined for college.

Case Study #2: A child grows up with both parents on drugs. He or she grows up and witnesses his or her mom have relationships with men. He or she hears stories about his or her father. He or she is forced to become a man or woman prematurely. His or her childhood was unstable and concerning. He or she was a constant nuisance at school. Is this his or her fault? I'm sure he or she wouldn't choose this life for him or herself. He or she is destined for death or the penitentiary.

Two things they both have in common are a mother's love, and **two things that their mothers will share are a mother's pain.**

Case Study #1 completes college and is blessed with material items that some adults who work 50 years cannot acquire. ***Case Study #2*** starts selling drugs because their love for themself and younger siblings is pressuring them to provide.

Case Study #1 knows that when times get hard, the child can always run to his or her family. ***Case Study #2*** knows that he or she doesn't have anyone to run to when times get hard.

Case Study #1 starts his or her life with a college degree and is on the way to a promising career. **Case Study #2** gets arrested for selling drugs and is beginning a lengthy prison sentence.

Case Study #1 is not hungry for success. He or she has peaked at an early age. He or she is content with just getting by. **Case Study #2** uses his or her incarceration to formulate a plan to start his or her own business so his or her children won't have to experience the harsh life he or she was born into.

Imagine if **Case Study #1 had Case study #2's** hunger, and realization that being independent was the only option. **What if Case Study #2 had Case Study #1**'s content personality. **Case Study #1 would be superb, and Case Study #2** would be asking for change at Rainbow Food & Liquors.

In conclusion, *always remember to remain humble and remember it is not how you start but how you finish. That will determine and define your legacy.*

Sincerely,
Antonius "Smooth" Finch

Antonius Finch

DEADLIEST DAY IN CHICAGO IN OVER A DECADE

Antonius Finch

DEADLIEST DAY IN CHICAGO OVER A DECADE

WEDNESDAY, SEPTEMBER 2, 2015, WAS THE DEADLIEST DAY in Chicago since July 5, 2003. I was horrified reading articles on this subject. I cringed when I read that an 11-year-old boy was killed. Ironically, my son turned 11 on September 2. I called my youngest son to hear his voice, and I called my oldest son's school to confirm he was safe. I can't imagine the amount of grief, sorrow, hurt and confusion parents feel when they lose a child to violence. I know the trauma that preys upon a family following a murder. I pray daily that I will never experience this.

The final statistics for September 2, 2015, is 9 deceased and 12 wounded. I thought about all of my loved ones I lost to violence. That is a tremendous toll left on those that are left to mourn the deceased. Feelings of guilt, depression, anger and rage may overtake some. As I think of everyone I lost to violence, I notice that nearly all of them share a common trait. They were all young, except for my Uncle Sam.

The first thing that comes to mind is identifying the issue. The issue is the loss of life among our youth. After identifying the problem, so many questions arise. Why were they at risk? What could they have done differently? Did we as a society fail them? What about their loved ones left behind? Those are only a few questions.

So please leave a comment on your personal opinion on what the problem is. I ask that if you identify an issue, please take a moment to offer a solution or any positive assistance!

    Respectfully,
    Antonius E. Finch

Antonius Finch

ACKNOWLEDGMENTS

I want to thank God for allowing me to achieve this goal. I'd also like to express gratitude to another author who I witnessed 1st hand sacrifice to complete her book, which became another source of motivation.

To my children, mom and dad, siblings, grandmother Brewer, uncles, aunts, cousins, friends, 7 Duece Murray Park family, Mike Oliver, Larry Wallace, and that Curie Condor brotherhood -- thank you for being instrumental in my life.

I also give thanks to John Snowden for being my photographer, SHE Publishing, LLC, for their collaboration in bringing this project to life and Michelle Phillips of CHELLD3 3D Visualization and Design for designing my book cover.

Antonius Finch

Thanks for reading this collection of short stories! Please let me know your thoughts by adding a Short review on Amazon and
[Finch Files – Englewood Spokesman (wordpress.com)](wordpress.com)*.*

Please continue to anticipate the next book "The Emasculation of Marriage!"

www.ingramcontent.com/pod-product-compliance
Lightning Source LLC
LaVergne TN
LVHW070436080526
838202LV00034B/2649